I Wish You Sanctity

Robert C. Broderick, KCHS

Illustrated by Virginia J. Broderick, LCHS

Our Sunday Visitor Publishing Division
Our Sunday Visitor, Inc.
Huntington, Indiana 46750

ISBN: 0-87973-432-9
LCCCN: 91-66663

PRINTED IN THE UNITED STATES OF AMERICA

Cover design by Virginia Broderick and Rebecca Heaston
Editorial production by Kelley Renz

432

Every morning lean thine arms awhile
Upon the windowsill of heaven
And gaze upon the Lord.
Then with the vision of thy heart
Turn strong to meet thy day.
—Author Unknown

Introduction

From where you stand and from where I stand, I can only wish the very best for you as I wish the same for myself. It is the ever-present and on-going quest for the better life for everyone that is the ambition of human living.

We all stand together in hope. Through this we borrow and use the strength that each person has in sufficiency for living. Hope combines our strengths and makes each one stronger in a unity of persons, a oneness of strength. What we wish for others, we wish for ourselves and by this we make the attainment of our goal, our salvation, more possible, not easier perhaps, but more likely of accomplishment. Hope also helps us to focus our individual sight on what is our own highest goal. It gives to community a "oneness," a unity of purpose, a goal for all to achieve while still acting for the best interest of one individual, namely oneself. It might be likened to communal selfishness.

People generally like to do things according to a formula. It simplifies everyday living. It is like forming a habit, it makes things easier to do and enables one to perform with more speed and satisfaction. For these reasons we all turn to special formulas for certain actions. Formulas are a help in understanding what we need for living effectively. These formulas range from recipes for food, exercise programs and diets to personal philosophies such as "honesty being the best policy" and formal prayer. It is a natural response to the intricate roles that each of us play in the routine of changing details and experiences of our everyday lives.

All of these formulated procedures, conscious and unconscious, are a fixed part of everyone's life. It is like saying "hello" when you answer the telephone, or "goodbye" when you finish the conversation. There is not much thought, the expression of genuine sincerity, in these habitual acts. We all tend to take them for granted even as we accept the words of a clerk or waitress who says "have a nice day!" after even the most brief encounter.

Many times these habitual acts are meant to be the quick completion of some action or the initiation of some project. They go on constantly in our lives, certainly to the benefit of ourselves and even at times to the good of others. They smooth the accomplishment of the generally accepted course of action described as "do unto others as you would have them do unto you." All of these to a degree satisfy the mandate of "love of neighbor," or achieve what passes in a simple manner for the practice of charity to all.

Somehow this does not really encompass all that we

would like to achieve. As we may deduce from the title of this book, there is a broader, more embracive extension of the admonition to love our neighbor as we love ourselves. It may be described simply as wishing for, actively seeking, and attaining the highest of spiritual good for ourselves and all others. It would be a formula that would achieve for everyone greater joy and satisfaction on earth and ultimately the greatest of happiness in the attainment of heaven in the life beyond all living.

Think for a moment what the gradual fulfillment of the wish that each one of us become sanctified would mean even in this life. There would be an end to harmful actions of injustice, murder, abuse of others, of war and want and the clash of hatred and terror and selfishness. There would be the generation of multiple smiles on the faces and peace in the lives of everyone.

This could be an encouragement to excellence in all persons. Especially in children — it would be a heaven-start program for them, leading them to seek higher standards in action, in ambitions, in the accomplishments of their lives. It would be a reward now as well as hereafter. It would replace the dangerous secular hierarchy of values with measures that would warrant greater self-esteem and personal satisfaction.

This would be rewarding for each one of us. Why? Because it would enable us to help to fulfill the will of God which each of us is encouraged and commanded to do. How? It would help each of us to bring about the salvific will of God. For God wills that every human being, from the moment of becoming a created person, be saved. This is what God intends for each one of us as the fullness of

His creative act. As Isaiah declared: "God created us all for His own glory."

God could do no less as Creator and we should do no less than make the effort to attain our own sanctity and that of all others. As St. Augustine proclaimed: "God wills all persons to be saved, not because there is no one who He does not wish saved, but because there is no one saved whose salvation He does not will." It is in fulfilling the will of God that we complete the communion of saints, a communion to which we all belong, to which we all aspire in order to obtain everlasting happiness. The real ambition of life is to be a saint for oneself. Failure is the overthrow of our purpose, hope, and desire. St. Thomas wrote in his *Disputations concerning Faith*, "Divine care supplies everybody with the means necessary for salvation, so long as he on his part does not put up obstacles."

Our part in fulfilling the salvific will of God, both for ourselves and for others, is in the personal, hopeful wish for holiness that we extend to others, actively and passively, and in our response to the means of obtaining this end. It is in seeking personally, both with and for others, a determined following of the Way, the Truth, and the Life. Every day on the Cross, God thirsts again for the souls of those to whom He has offered the eternal drink of truth. And there is a formula which we can make effective with both silent prayer and with speech. It is one which we can actively seek for others by more than saying, "Goodbye," which means "God be with you," but rather wishing everyone we meet and greet, "I wish you sanctity!"

Love one another as I have loved you

1 A quick glance at the world and its people may lead one to believe that the fashion of the day lies in trying *not* to be nice. It sometimes seems that it is fashionable not to be good, kind, or thoughtful, and that the only satisfying enterprise is a sinful one. To add to this by asserting that nobody really wants to be good is the folly of personal defeatism. To attempt to live in such a manner, to follow that fashion, is the true waste of life.

This need not be. This should not be, especially among all who profess to be more than the animals, or who realize that they are intended for higher, more noble actions and achievements. What does this mean? Does it merely claim that virtue is a reproach to vice, and is so recognized and applauded? Or does it declare that there is in all human life a spiritual something, a longing, a perpetual thirst that must be satisfied if life is to be lived wholly, completely?

Everyone reaches toward final certainty of accomplishment, of obtaining a goal that gives life meaning and personal value. We think all life, each individual life has such purpose. We affirm for ourselves and others that arising from all the harsh realities of life there is a purposeful meaning and a natural inclination to progress back to the great reality of our creation. There is within us an innate desire, an all-consuming will to return to our Creator, to be reunited with the One who made us and wills that we be one forever with the Goodness who not only made us but sustains our every step in our journey to Him. As Pope Pius XI proclaimed: "The saints have ever been, are, and ever will be the greatest benefactors of society, and perfect models for every class and profession, for every state and condition of life, from the simple and uncultured peasant to the master of science and letters, from the humble artisan to the commander of armies, from the father of a family to the ruler of peoples and nations, from simple maidens and matrons of the domestic hearth to queens and empresses" (*Divinus Illus. Magistri*, Dec. 1929).

In responding to this inner urge, this seeking of ultimate completion, we have definite aids for its attainment. These begin with faith, for it is faith that gives everyone understanding and direction. Faith alone brings spiritual affinity, a bonding of persons through a shared desire and effort to assure mutual aid and progress toward the final end for each and all, fulfillment that is called salvation, the ultimate oneness with Christ. This brings all life, the life of everyone in Christ, to its fullness of meaning. The one, grand mission of life is to be finally transcendent, to be perfected, to be united with Christ, to possess heaven and its eternal happiness. The wishing of sanctity for another, this oneness with Christ, is in reality wishing that good for ourselves as well. It is total unselfishness for we cannot love and at the same time not wish the goodness and sanctity of the other. It is the love extension, the going-outward essential to all loving.

Examples surround us in everything we do. We cannot love without loving, cannot be loved without loving. We cannot seek our own good without seeking the good of others. We cannot seek perfection unless we also seek the perfection of others — no one can replicate a good without that good being again and again its own reward, especially when this is perceived in others. The truth as truth is a fixed star, it gives direction to our every action on behalf of our neighbor, and loving our neighbor we love ourselves.

We can love ourselves only when we do not hurt ourselves by sin. There can be no genuine sorrow, no penance, nor remedy for sin unless we love — first, love of God, then love of ourselves, and love by which we wish for and seek the good, the sanctity, the final happiness of everyone. It was John of Salisbury who said in the twelfth century: "Public welfare which fosters the state and its individual citizens consists in sanctity of life, for life is man's most cherished possession and its sanctity his greatest blessing."

It is through the expression in action of our love for our neighbor that we can almost without thinking, help ourselves. It is in this way that we can seek the mercy of God for others and for ourselves.

We truly express our affection when we, by mind and will, provide for, seek out, and attain the well-being of another, our neighbor. It is through this communication of our love of Christ that we also assert our love of self and love of neighbor. By projecting the desire to another for the same sanctity we wish for ourselves, we reaffirm our love of God and cooperate to fulfill His will. It is this that God intended when He created each of us.

We give glory to God when we attain for ourselves and for others the salvation that is in the mind of God. It makes of humanity a community, by giving it a unity of effort and intention. When we wish the good for ourselves, we must wish it for all others to fulfill what God wills for each. This gives value to each and every act we do. It perfects each act and leads all to perfection. The author, Robert H. Benson, wrote: "Holiness seeks to propagate itself, becoming love as it does so, and cries out, 'Be holy, for I am holy.'"

We would find it difficult indeed to think of human love without extending that love to the fullest, its ultimate reality. Thus a person who loves and marries must also wish salvation, sanctity for the one loved. When two people beget and produce a child, it would be monstrous if they would not at the same time wish with all their hearts for that child to live close to the loving Creator, the child's sanctity. The outcome of every simple human effort must be to achieve the well-being of all, and most assuredly of those we love. We would indeed be reduced in ourselves if we were to seek anything less. The very foundation of all being, of all living, is in the First Cause who is the Maker of us all and the source of all our actions for good. St. Thomas says, "Not to go along the way to God is to go back" (*Comment on Ephesians*).

all things are brought to perfection through Christ

2 The phrase "one for all and all for one" may be a romantic and adequate democratic call, but it falls short of our inner yearning — the desire to be ourselves in excellence. The one-for-all, all-for-one thinking is sufficient to keep us in the rut of sameness, of mediocrity but not at all adequate if we want to realize our full potential to achieve more, to attain what God wants everyone to be — that is, a saint among all, and a saint among saints.

This is attainable, this is real. We do not vote ourselves into perfection. It is arduous, but each of us is free to pursue this goal. It is humanly feasible and within our reach to aspire to and attain sanctity. We seek this for ourselves, we seek this for everyone in the extension of charity. Do not limit God by the yardstick measure of the world, nor by a bankbook or medals. Providence is the full design of life made by living, dying, and attaining salvation. To this we direct our love, our mind, and all our effort.

In life truth is our fixed star. By this we plot the course of our life. We begin with love which imbues us with strengths that we never fully realize until we give them direction, a resolve, a purpose. As St. John declared so vividly, so directly: "God is love and he who abides in love abides in God and God in him" (I Jn. 4:16). We know the greatest of the virtues of life is charity, that is, love. And love is extending, all-embracing, going out to creatures and to the Creator. As a child loves the natural father and mother, so humans must recognize the love of the Creator through whom we have our very being.

There is no greater gift of charity than the gift of life. The giving of life is God's first gift of love to each of us. To refuse that gift is our greatest rebellion, the sinful rejection of God's will as the Creator. Because life expresses God's infinite charity to humans, its denial is the most frightening insult to and rejection of God's love. To reject, to prevent God's love toward and for another human being is to stand arrogant in the path of God — it is to fling back His love in the most vicious, unreasonable manner, the supreme insult a human, dependent being, can give to his or her God-Creator.

The horror of this act is that it is the cause of great sorrow — for it interferes with, it blocks our primary response to God, a response of cooperative love. Only because we have faith in our Creator and in His love for us, can we in turn show love, first, toward God himself, and secondly, toward our neighbor, other human beings, for the love of God. It is only in this manner that we can realize for ourselves and others the final rewarding happiness that God intended for each of us in His creative act whereby He gave us life.

It was for this total fulfillment, this ever-loving good that God created us, redeemed us, and continues to support us with unending grace — even the grace of our every breath. His gifts to us strengthen us to do His will. Our gifts in return prove our love for Him. Recognizing His will for others, we can help them to fulfill God's will for all through love. It is thus that the circle of love returns to complete and replenish the glory of our God.

This fulfillment we know can only come about through faith. By living our faith we begin to draw together the circle of love, for ourselves and for our neighbor. St. John of the Cross wrote: "He that loves not his neighbor abhors God." And St. John the Evangelist declared: "One who has no love for his brother he has seen cannot love the God he has not seen" (1 Jn. 4:20).

We all must strive to attain the spiritual kingdom. This ultimate achievement is the objective of us all, for all were intended to be saints of heaven in the will and love of God by the right of our birth. It was the philosopher Jacques Maritain who said, "Sainthood is not the negation of life." No, it is the beginning, for it is in the very will of our Creator, "the kingdom prepared for you from the creation of the world" (Mt. 25:34). We are all heirs of the same kingdom, heirs of the same promise of God our Creator, who has fashioned this home of our promise for all who believe and serve in love.

Besides this spiritual kingdom, there is first or also an interior kingdom. It is, in a sense, a social kingdom inhabited by men and women of good will, the friends of God. All who are heirs, the sons and daughters of God, whose spiritual relationships to God in carrying out His will, eventually will come together in glory. We all share together in hope, a lively hope. No one can be numb to such hope and still live a fruitful life that will earn heaven.

But while we live in hope, clinging to the hems of garments worn by those who have attained their rewards, we must serve in this world. We must carry on the works of God in His world, a world which He also created in love. Even here our heaven can begin, for our reward will really commence when we, in the earnest dignity of living the will of God, strive for our perfection, as our God is perfect. We know we will need to renounce many things, but this we do also out of love. The dead leaves of sin and selfishness must fall from the tree of our lives before we can grow anew.

God is Father of us all. We renounce only ourselves by giving ourselves freely to God. In a union of goodness and love, we became worthy branches of the Vine. And we have helps beyond our limited strengths that aid us if we but seek them in prayer: the evangelical virtues of voluntary poverty, chastity, and obedience — these are all the services of love.

There is also a renunciation that is required by the love of neighbor which we accept with resignation for the love of God (cf. Mt. 22:37-40). This is extended beyond our love of self and to do this there must be a giving up of self-ish pursuits that would exclude other humans from our generosity. Thus, love of God accelerates through prayer and self-denial and in turn begets love of neighbor. It progresses with some speed after we learn from God that the yoke, the burden God gives to us, is not too burdensome when one is compassionate and humble (Mt. 11:28-29).

As a follow-up of this love of neighbor, there flows an abundance of grace brought about by devout prayer which engenders and renews the love of God. Our prayer should be a continuing exercise. It is the OS formula (*ora semper*) which means pray always. The ancient Gaelic people adopted praying almost as a habit, a day-in and day-out expression of the love they felt for their Creator. They found a simple but comprehensive kind of prayer such as: "I in your path, O God, and Thou God in my steps." To this everyday salute to God, walking in the way of God and being assured and confident that God will be beside each person, they often added a thought that was a part of their common work and play, "God help my handling." This gave a spiritual dimension to everything they did, and God's help made each task, each game easier and more rewarding.

Faith, Hope and the Love of God turn conflict to peace - turn death to eternal life

3 The misfortune of misfortunes of our time, more than other times, is that sins are committed against other humans by humans because of a broad spectrum of misapplied intentions. It is faulty moral thinking and bad rationalizing, resulting in the flaunting of God's plan and intent for all of us. Being holy because God is holy is not at all acceptable in today's society — it is ignored.

There are today sins of economics — cheating, dishonesty, false accounting, theft. There are sins against the society of individuals — rape, incest, adultery, fornication, the failures of marriages, the rejection of vows and of simple honor. There arc the gross and hideous sins of murder and violence, of child abuse, terrorism, of devilish cults and obscene practices. There are sins against nature — the fouling of the land and waters, the indifference to and torture of animals. All of these and more, but the great misfortune is that each sin is committed by humans against humans. It is the bitten-hand of ingratitude and the finger of shame against the dignity of all mankind.

It is almost beyond what love can bear. There must be more that mortal and rational human beings can do to live up to what God expects of His created handiwork. There must be a higher equation possible or lives and minds will be wasted, lost forever.

Many of the gifted, the rich, are too proud to give a pittance or two, to benefit the wretched, the sinned-against. But worse than this, they will not so much as stir their minds to uplift themselves. The wanton waste of goodness is where pride provides the giver with abundant gifts, but he shows only crumbs of compassion. The too brief glow of a tossed coin has little effect on the vice or sin that caused the need or wrought the want. A pittance cannot be a claim to the reward for charity. Where there is passing pity and no real love of neighbor, there is only the swagger of false charity. No one can claim to be a worthy saint whose footprints cannot readily be seen along the pathway, whose charity has not been a beacon for others. The one who humbly moves along the quiet way of service, of love, of charity given, stands in the end with the light about him and his soul in eternal sunshine.

With even a minuscule pause to think, we can each realize that goodness is being alive to the love of God and neighbor. No matter what the moment's work or pleasure, we are aware enough to ask ourselves, "Is this our treasure? Is this the will of God for us?"

We can decide in the sunlight of faith that we will and must abandon all other idols in our lives, be they persons, success, sexual gratifications, money, or other material possessions. It is then that we realize along with Dante who saw most clearly: "Everything is at its best and most perfect when in the condition intended for it by the First Cause, which is God" (*Monarchy*).

This is our hope, attainable as God willed it to be for each person. We thus must think of ourselves and of each other, "looking to others' interests rather than our own" (Ph. 2:4). This then helps us to shun sins against others and we hear St. Paul's admonition "to work with anxious concern to achieve your salvation" (Ph. 2:12-15), for it is God who brings to birth in us the desire for attaining the will of God. We empty ourselves of sinful concerns and are filled with hope for ourselves and others by obtaining a new outlook on values. We look at and see the world about us, and others standing near to us in a new light, the Light that is Christ.

We realize that for the majority of us the very word *sainthood* is an uncomprehended word — we shun it even if we understand it because of what it implies. The poet Francis Thompson has given it meaning: "Sainthood is the touch of God. To most, even good people, God is a belief. To the saint He is an embrace. They have felt the wind of His locks, His heart has beaten against their sides. They do not believe in Him, for they know Him" (*Sanctity and Song*).

Sanctity will bring to us and within us great changes.

There will be a new wisdom worthy of us concerning our attitude toward our bodies — how we understand and use the gifts of sex that God created. There will be a change in our spirit, a change which will bring peace beyond our understanding for we will look at people and all things with a new and profound intensity. Above all we will begin to seek the things that are higher (Col. 3:2), of greater value in reaching toward our salvation and that of others.

We will realize for perhaps the first time that we are, each one of us, sacred. We are chosen by God our Creator to be holy and to be the beloved of God (Col. 3:11ff). Because of this destiny we have great dignity and worth, and having this we now must act with mercy and kindness to ourselves and others. We must put on love, wearing it as a shield of protection from the world and the worldly. This assures us of peace for we have been created for that peace from the very first (Col. 3:12-17).

With this realization we come to look upon ourselves as persons who were created worthy to be saints. We understand how we can be "temples of God" because as St. Paul declares, God dwells in us (I Cor. 3:17). Consequently we begin to do all for God, acting for His glory (I Cor. 10:31) that we may all come to our promised glory for which we were created. Because of this indwelling of God, we must look upon ourselves differently than in the past. We are not slugs, failures, outcasts. We take on new strengths, new and higher directions: "Whoever is joined to the Lord becomes one spirit with him" (I Cor. 6:17).

This spiritual aspect that we can recognize in ourselves lifts each of us to a new level, making it possible to move toward an honest feeling of worth. We can describe ourselves in true fellowship with Christ. We can "put on the mind of Christ" (Ph. 2:5). We cease to think of ourselves as selfish individuals whose only purpose is to serve ourselves. Instead we can now give of ourselves, emptying ourselves out of love for others. And we can transform the world, making it a "vesting-room" for the pageant of love and glory that is ours and our neighbors' by right of creation.

As we seek the wisdom which is meant to adorn our minds, a renewed regard for the sacredness of our bodies comes to us. We see a new, more religious path that leads the spirit to holiness of life. Through this we "Do not conform to this age but are transformed by a renewal of mind, and discern what is the will of God" (Rom. 12:2).

We as individuals are together as one in the passage to perfection, the course toward sanctity. Among us, love ricochets as we share the faith that gives us strength. We will gradually cease to be "loose canons" aimlessly flailing at the world and its pleasures, and become true actors with a sure purpose and new resolve.

The Lord says "who lives in me will bear much fruit"

4 By instinct we are inclined to run after the pleasures and fleshpots of this world — it is everyone's weakness, nature's original blight. But in creating us, God's stated intent was for us to live not for this world, but for the world to come, for a perfect existence in glory and for His glory. This should be our aim, our special enterprise. For this we seriously strive, for it is vain to seek anything other than God. Now we live in the shadows which do not reveal the world to come. But we can, with faith, go forward, trusting in the light which will be the brilliance of God's glory. It is God's will to sanctify us. It is only with the assistance of Him who strengthens us that we can

begin and persist in our journey toward perfection.

There are many helps which make it possible for us to realize sanctity for ourselves and others. The poet Francis Thompson said, "Short arm needs man to reach to heaven, so ready is heaven to stoop to him" (*Grace of the Way*). God, it may be said, has a great investment in each one of us whom he has created to walk His world. His investment will pay dividends when we submit our wills to His and are perfected. Each of us, still moist with baptism's primal waters, turn from the font and spring into action. We may stumble, stagger, and firmly set our wills against the great tides of grace. But better still, we can choose to break away into grandeur, to find the brilliance of the promise that is ours if we hold up our cups to the fullness of the divine bounty.

We have the means of moving toward the promised prize, with our sights fixed on the goal. Beyond all ambition, aspiration, all assurance, beyond the two-plus-two-are-four thinking of this world there stands a truth more true. As easy as turning a stone, anyone can find God — His comfort, His strength. The poet Francis Thompson says: "In life we wade the waves of mud, we plunge heart-deep among the fronds of desire and we emerge a lily-white vessel ready to be filled with grace and life eternal." This is more than the promise in the bud, this is the final possession we seek as our own. We live the Life because the Life lives in us. It is our one destiny — all our longing. We might say this is our treasure, the enriched end that God prepared for us when He created us. God said to the prophet Jeremiah, "Before I formed you in the womb I knew you, before you were born I dedicated you. . ." (Jer.

1.5). The gracious, loving hand of God is always stretched out to us, to aid and save us, to bring us to himself.

We are engaged in the great enterprise of life. Since each of us is a holy temple, it is for us to give witness to the Christ who lives in us (Ph. 2:5; Gal. 2:20). We do this by showing our love of God and neighbor (I Cor. 4:16). What we do compounds God's investment in us, for God is life — we live in His light and love. It is His spirit of truth that enlightens and strengthens each one of us. (Jn. 14:26; 15:26; 16:7-15). And it is this Light, enlightening us (Jn.1:9; 8:12) that makes us shine like gold for all to see, and to prove that we may become the profit accruing to God's investment. He is the good Banker, the good Shepherd (Jn. 10:11). We are the nourished branches of the Vine that is Christ (Jn. 15:1-5).

We are in turn shown the Way, by making ourselves the Way (Jn. 14:6). We each can follow more securely, more assuredly, because God lives in us (Jn. 17:23). And because of our love of God, we love our neighbor (Jn. 14:21; 1 Jn. 4:12-17; 20-21) and earn an everlasting investment in our neighbor's glory and our own.

How can we do this? Simply by making sacrifices of the things that hold us back from God. Sacrifice leads to love. It is love. It is the learned art of unselfishness. This gradually gives to us the ability to love ourselves and others for the love of God. We grow away from a mere animal existence and raise our activities to a higher, spiritual level, to the heights of mind and will. And this is the progression toward a flowering resurrection of the soul, our eternal happiness, our unique individual happiness that God intended for us.

We may sometimes look at our weaknesses, our pains and the continuing hardships we must overcome, and be tempted to lose heart. But strength is all about us, surrounding us. If there is pain in life, it is an aspect of love's mystery. God is with us in all His enduring love — it is our fault alone if we turn away from Him, thinking that if we have Him we cannot have anything else, whereas we have been given all for our use and gain. God is like the sun that drinks up every tear. It may be a painfully slow process, but we can only approach the majesty of immortal glory when we have first risen to sanctity.

Take up the compass of spiritual love and the needle will always point to God. It is one-directional in guiding us to our greatest joy. God's love for us is both chain and anchor, our sure connection to the hope we cherish. We alone chose each link of love and tether ourselves to Him. To be unaware of the very source of love is likened to our trying to pour water upward. We need not be afraid nor discouraged. We must not let our hearts be the tomb of all our hopes. Rather, we must rise, enlivened by the Love that is attentive to us. The sands of remembered pains and faults have silt up our hearts where they turn us aside from our Creator. We need not be an arid waste, but look to the fresh beauty that we are in the dignity of our being.

We must know ourselves for what we are. Not to admit our weaknesses is the blindness imposed by folly. We must be honest about our faults and not put them away to be addressed some future day. Reckon with them now. For the spirit grows robust with the effort to exercise virtue.

It takes time and thought for us, imperfect as we are, to realize that the Creator-God planted us in the world and provided all the rich nutrients necessary for us to bud and bloom into beings lovelier than the angels. It is such a great expectation that one should prepare for the arduous journey along the way. We each have the aids, the means, only we must use them wisely, drawing from the source of all wisdom. The Psalmist declares:

Yet with you I shall always be;
you have hold of my right hand;
With your counsel you guide me,
and in the end you will receive me in glory.
Whom else have I in heaven?
And when I am with you, the earth delights me not.
Though my flesh and my heart waste away,
God is the rock of my heart and my portion forever.
—Ps. 73:23-26

The wonder is that even by denial, we may pursue the greatest good, making love out of every misfortune and sacrifice.

The food of the saints is love. It quickens, it gives life, it nourishes, it embraces all with the joy of living for God and others. Be assured God has made in us a great investment, and to think that we alone can become the final profit, the glory in the granary of God, is to realize that in God's accounting, we count most. It will be our greatest blessing to one day complete the circle from God to God.

All the songs, all the symphonies of the world are concerted into the one harmony which is heaven. All the trillings of song-birds are but the faintest echoes of the hosannahs of heaven — and we may someday hear and be delighted by the deluge of sound that will forever caress our senses.

The roadway to sanctity is often silent, but not always a lonely road, not when we travel together, with each other's help. We can wish for sanctity for everyone and be willing to assist them and ourselves. But for many people, sainthood is incomprehensible, it is foreign to the spirit of the world, too self-demanding, too hard a course to follow.

Each one of us has known God, perhaps in pain. We have found Him there and learned that the clean-burning flame somehow purifies. We have experienced that in the struggle we are made strong, and we know that the love that surrounds us, even if it is a purgatorial love, raises us up again and again. We know our strength is really not from ourselves as we confront our weaknesses; we instead are all too aware of the forged chains of divine love. This we know is considered foolishness to many, but to us it is both weapon and armor because we put on Christ when we love like Christ.

Men and women, garlanded with the beauty and blessings of the world, can flaunt all of it and dare to sow noxious weeds among the glory-blossoms of God's garden. All of nature, all of the fruits and seeds thereof, the Creator-God fashioned for us on the garden-looms of earth. This is where we are meant to seek and find our destiny and final dignity. But we too often take and destroy — we do not know how to accept with true joy the garment of finest array. We fashion a sin-woven cloth of faithless despair, although we have the means, the abundant nourishment, to make a vesture of beauty.

The Creator made it possible for us to take into our

grasp the great bounty of God's gifts. It is simple — as Dante said, "That, what God willeth, that we also will." To do the will of God, to become saints among saints, to follow Him in everything, to try to be like Him is the one certain course to take in doing His will.

Poet Joseph M. Plunkett from his anteroom of ill health could express this recognition of God:

I see His blood upon the rose
And in the stars the glory of His eyes
His body gleams amid eternal snows,
His tears fall from the skies.
I see His face in every flower;
The thunder and the singing of the birds
Are but His voice — and carven by His power,
Rocks are His written words.
All pathways by His feet are worn,
His strong heart stirs the everlasting sea,
His crown of thorns is twined with every thorn,
His cross is every tree.

Lord, prosper
the work
of our
hands

VB

5 We have all drunk too much of the world. We are intoxicated with the beauties and the bright goodness about us. God has given us heady wine from the bounteous winepress that is His alone to give, and we have learned to use it only to our own undoing. Why can we not learn to use it to our advantage? Why can we not reverse that course and begin to use God's mighty gifts and graces to our own proper ends, to become what we were intended and created to be? Why must we always act perversely, coiling the asp of delight about our beautiful gifts, becoming the slaves of our own nature, the breakers of our own vessels of hope and joy?

We can begin to use the blessings given to us to heal, to strengthen, to replenish repeatedly our own powers of living. If carnal love and delight is our main fare, then we will soon feed on left-overs, and the meats and fruits of true joy will not satisfy us but will instead be ever tasteless. Even maturity will not find any good in the foul and withered fruits. Our dignity and honor are not located in the shook-crumbs of yesterday's feast. Instead we can all be full with the fullness of God, renewed from His bounty through love. We each as a single unit may become one with Him who is the sum of all units, the whole integrity of all being in Christ.

We have often spoken about the means we possess to bring about change that is like a continuing fresh tide flowing into the ocean of love about us. It is not always an easy thing, the management of our minds and bodies. We can exercise the body to build up muscle and sinew. We can even play games to tighten up a slack mind. But too often the inferior quality of our lives is not due to what we think is weakness but to what it lacks in moral fiber. It is spiritual disuse that often brings on the real pain of living.

One way of bringing about full, spiritual health is through prayer — it is prayer that binds the fibers of the soul and makes the graces of God effective. "All that should be sought for in the exercise of prayer is conformity of our will with the divine will, in which consists the highest perfection," says St. Teresa. And St. John of the Cross warns, "He that flees from prayer flees from all that is good."

Worldly people, the savants of pleasure, the hoydens of the moment, have a profound distaste for prayer of any kind. They find it humiliating, too abrasive of their egos. They think it can in no way be a power providing the medicine of true spiritual remedy. For the modern seeker after pleasure to value such a thing as prayer, he would have to know it and not knowing it he cannot evaluate it as either remedy or aid. And for bodies that are abused and pampered there is no admission of the need for a remedy — the medicine is not valued or comprehended by the spoon on which it rides.

It is ignorance of prayer that frightens. It is not knowing Christ that makes it seem difficult for us to become one with Him. In Scripture St. John leads the way clearly for us: "Through him all things came into being, and apart from him nothing came to be. Whatever came to be in him, found life, life for the light of men. The light shines on in the darkness, a darkness that does not overcome it" (Jn. 1:3-5). This suggests that we can find our way to the greater good for which we were created. We can seek to unite ourselves with Christ through prayer, a constant among the wavering inconstancies of living (cf. Lk. 18:1; Mk. 14:38). By being united with Christ, we can become more like Christ, the perfect union of the one with the Whole, the created with the Creator. It is through prayer that we establish fellowship with God and with our neighbor. It forms the paving blocks for the road to sanctity.

Prayer itself is a desire for perfection for it proclaims our wish and intention to become a better person. The perfect prayer is the *Lord's Prayer* — the *Our Father*. (cf. Mt. 6:9; Lk. 11:2ff). It is the embodiment of all aspects of prayer — it raises the mind to God, it is the petition which seeks our needs from God's beneficence, it places us in an attitude of homage to God and shows our willingness to grow in holiness for the glory of God. It is also a request for the graces that are necessary for sanctification and holiness. When we pray alone or with others we follow the urging of St. Paul that "with one heart and voice you may glorify God, the Father of our Lord, Jesus Christ" (Rm. 15:6).

There also is a special need and urging to pray quietly, alone, fulfilling the words of our Lord on the necessity of "praying always and not losing heart" (Lk. 18:1). This can be done by saying as often as we wish a simple prayer, for example, "Lord Jesus Christ, Son of God, Savior, have mercy on me a sinner." Or we may make a habit of saying a prayer of love: "Jesus, with all your saints I love you." For prayer is an on-going action of the heaven-bound, as St. Paul tells us: "whether you eat or drink —whatever you do — do all for the glory of God" (I Cor. 10:31). And St. Augustine writes: "Let the harmony of your life ever rise as a song, so that you may never cease to praise God's glory." St. Thomas adds: "Man prays so long as he directs his whole life toward God." Therefore we must never forget as Father Charles Olier reminds us: "Jesus Christ is within both ourselves and our works to fill all our faculties with His own Self"(*Catechism of Internal Life*).

We must turn toward what vivifies us, to the source of our being and our strength. The weaknesses we have because of our physiognomy may be useful in gaining greater spiritual health. But a moral weakness cannot be exercised away, there is no weight-lifting or jogging program to correct a sloppy moral physique. There is no diet that removes the blubber caused by unrestrained indulgence. It seems quite evident to every thinking person that there is a "law of sin." It goes something like this, "you sin, you pay," and to refurbish a moral wreck requires a rigorous course of discipline in restraint, in obedience, in patience. One cannot do one good act, refrain but once from a stupid sin and think that is a balanced diet to make one whole again, just as the forsaking of one candy bar will not bring about a svelte body. Virtue demands a strong, forthright exercise of repression and control if it is to gain a vitality.

The most certain diet, the single most effective way to a sound spiritual body is to feast with Christ. We have said the food of saints is love — it is the real source of strength. Our moral integrity has been made weak and flaccid by luxurious living and devitalization. Many of us are moral cripples. We need a few turns with bar-bells of a more ascetic life, a mortifying of what we have claimed as our right to indulge ourselves to exhaustion. We neither love ourselves, nor anyone, and we seldom think with respect of either Christ or neighbor. By what right, what freedom that is ours, dare we take up drugs that rob us of our minds, cripple our wills, and fill our souls with hate? How dare we hate another person to the extent of torturing and maiming his or her body and soul?

How can one claim to be following the path of Christian love, while one steals what is precious to his neighbor? How can one force another to put on the hair-shirt of suffering when the consequential blood clots into stiffness on the moral flesh of every other human being? And seeing another's weakness, the horror of pain that cramps his very soul, how can we say we are free when his pain is also ours? Are we not affected, caught up in anyone's and everyone's moral ill-health? The scented sins of modern life can never hide with perfume the body of desiccated and rotten indulgence. Our claimed freedom to sin is evil, carrion strewn on the fields of life. If we choose sin because our minds rationalize it as rectitude then it will take a strenuous exercise of love to even think of recovery, of regained well-being.

But it is God, our Lover, who says: "Arise, my beloved, my beautiful one, and come!" (Sg. 2:10) It is He who has care of us and His world, "The Holy Ghost over the bent world broods with warm breast and with ah! bright wings" (Gerald Manley Hopkins).

Now in science, the culture of medicine, the new insights into the brain and its workings have borne out the immense value of the law of love. And often the body, sin-weakened, will yet prove that one's strength is not in the tissues or muscles but in the control by love in the mind and soul. We transcend nature only through love of God and neighbor. The poet Francis Thompson wrote; "Sanctity is genius in religion; the saint lives for and in religion, as the man of genius lives for and in his peculiar attainment. Nay, it might be said that sanctity is the supreme form of genius, with the great difference that sanctity is dependent on no special privilege —or curse — of temperament. Both are the outcome of man's inner and individual love, and are characterized by an eminent fervor, which is the note of love in action" (*Health and Holiness*).

It may be painful far us to think about the austere changes that love of God and neighbor require. But it is the right and simple thing to do, the difficult struggle is all in the beginning. When we apply, take on ourselves, the law of loving charity, we become the law. It becomes a part of us, it grows easier and more pleasant. Our minds and wills begin the steady journey along the path to greater personal peace. This is the peace that alone is real, the peace given to us by the Prince of Peace. John the apostle writes of this Prince's words, "Peace is my farewell to you, my peace is my gift to you; I do not give it to you as the world gives peace" (Jn. 14:27).

From the angels' song at the birth of that Prince to His departure, we are assured that from Love comes love without causing any bodily conflicts. We can be at peace even as we take up spiritual arms against the coiled enemy that fights within us. We can call upon the strength of God's love for us. We know that sometimes we go the way of weaklings, too feeble to seek help, too lazy to even struggle out of the ooze of vanity, too selfish in our sins of frivolity to accept help. We lack human dignity and easily succumb to petty sins and omissions that vitiate our spirits.

Our noble minds cringe and seek the grotesque, the un-reasoned course of action such as dictated by cults and devilish beliefs. We know where the remedy lies. The medicines of the soul are closer, more available than the nostrums of our medicine cabinets. Our hope and health of spirit is fixed by the chain of love which joins us to our Creator-God. How can we refuse the certain help, the ever-saving power of a creed of love and faith?

This brings us back to prayer, the aerobic practice of mind and heart, exercise that will make us strong in love. We must begin to pray for the grace to become whole again in body and spirit. St. Paul wrote: "Prayer of this kind is good, and God our Savior is pleased with it, for He wants men to be saved and come to know the truth" (I Tm. 2:3ff).

We are certain that we are loved or we would not exist. We were made to be eternally loved. To know we are the object of God's love should give each one of us such a feeling of importance, such an uplifting of dignity, of individual grandeur, a feeling of being unique in the complex world, that we should fall down in utter subjection to this love. We alone are the pot of gold at the end of God's rainbow of love. What joy, what recognition, what exaltation is ours, the Creator's crowning good. Our aim must be to take advantage of redemption through a return of love.

Look around you at your world of rippling streams, of sun-dazzled west and the incipient glory of dawn that walks down the lark's ladder of song into a new day. Give no thought to the nagging of any kind of despair. "God is seen in everything, O world invisible, we know thee, O world unknowable, we know thee, inapprehensible we clutch thee!" the poet Thompson wrote. And we can be certain that God is in each one of us, and each is brother or sister to all other masterpieces of our Creator-God. All are in Christ who is the Vine and we are the branches, entwined in love, taking strength and grace from the Source of Love.

The love of God has been poured into our hearts by his Spirit

6 Exercise, every one knows, makes for a strong and healthy body. But what of the spirit, the soul? It too requires some training, some stretching of the muscles, some pulling against resistance, to make it strong and supple. Wouldn't it be wonderful if there were health centers, clubs where one could go and work out to improve the soul's fitness? Some of course will reply, "Oh we do have such places: churches, bible-study classes, revivals, retreats, religion in the great stone houses of Christendom" — yes, all of these, the whole galaxy of neglected and spurned sources of mind-renewal. But what is there for the individual, the Creator-made man and woman who

sorely lacks quality of life? They need something to invigorate, quicken the wine-like fluids of God's grace within them even while they are bound by the pleasures and all the false lures of the material world. Can we not do some aerobic praying and gain greater spiritual robustness and agility? Happily the body is somehow made more able, more nimble, more awesome by a quickening of the spiritual life. It borrows from divine love, enriching itself, and becomes newly sensitive to the spiritual forces, the muscle-making machines of God.

In this way all of society can be rejuvenated, the whole becoming stronger as the strength of each individual is increased. We cannot call a virtue such as chastity or patience a foe of the mind and body when we assess the ruthless consequences of its absence. It is in the cultivation of the spiritual by the individual that the democratic thinking and acting of each person for his or her own good can bring about not only his or her good but also the good of society. It is thus that holiness energizes. We can readily see, if we make the first, small step, that holiness heals, strengthens, that our virtue increases from virtue. We can realize that our weakness gains strength in the love of God when we turn away from the horrors that accompany the absence of moral sanity. We do not become ascetic freaks when we accept the divine will; rather, we become stronger. The strength of sanctity becomes the sanctity of power. The repetition of a prayerful act, as in physical exercise, increases health. Only in this manner can everyone reach a resurrected spiritual power, the God-willed power.

Indeed there are opportunities galore, aids and means both sacramental and spiritual, to help us acquire this health of soul. Chiefly to be considered are seven fitness aids, like machines in a health club — these are known to us as the seven gifts of the Holy Spirit, the Spirit of God sent to us to give us greater flexibility, greater stamina to gain sanctity. He gives light to our mind, enflames our heart and makes firm our will.

These seven gifts are: *wisdom, understanding, knowledge, counsel, piety, fortitude, and fear of the Lord.* The exercise of these as habits, perfects those virtues, those powers, whereby each of us can aspire to and obtain sanctity, fulfilling God's will for us.

We must admit that we have frequently become negligent and indolent in using the sinews of mind and will. We let our spiritual muscles atrophy by non-use and misuse. It can become a veritable malady that demands the most radical conversion in some instances and in others the gentler remedy of "giving-it-another-try." In the Church, the Advocate, the Gift-giver, the Spirit is always with us and present. We need but to open ourselves in prayer to take advantage of these potent aids we have available to us.

In this age that has for too long been occupied with the "good of the many," providing a democratic abundance of goods, now finds that what is needed more is attention to the individual to bring about a union of powers and potentialities.

Look around you and you will see that we need the love of neighbor along with divine charity. It is in this that the community idea really functions. And it succeeds best, most advantageously, when we apply the Gifts of the Holy Spirit to ourselves and to the benefit of our neighbor, especially those nearest and dearest to us. It is in this manner that we can best elicit their help and give help to them.

Not working out in any particular order, we shall begin with a few turns of exercise in *fortitude*. This is not an exercise that makes one a stand-out hero. Instead, just consider traveling in an airplane, circling the airport, waiting for the fog to lift, an icy freeway, waiting in line for some material good — these are enough to try the fortitude of the body. But it is in the soul that we must exercise the real fortitude of present day living. We must assault the fortress of the world, the alluring, tempting excessive goods that modern life presents. In order to say *no*! we need fortitude, strength beyond our will, a strength of mind. Francis Thompson rightly declared "The body (I might say) is immersed in the soul, as a wick is dipped in oil; and its flame of active energy is increased or diminished by the strength or weakness of the fecundizing soul. But this oil, this soul, is enriched a hundred fold by the infusion of the Holy Spirit; the human will is intensified by union with the Divine Will; and for the flame of human love or active energy is substituted the intense flame of Divine Love or Divine Energy. Rather, it is not a substitution, but the higher is added to the lower, the lesser augmented by and contained within the greater. The effective energies of the fleshly wick, the body, are correspondingly and immensely augmented." (*Health and Holiness*).

By making use of the power of the Divine Spirit, we can exercise our will to act with fortitude, striding everywhere. The quicksands of weakness no longer hinder us; we can turn away from the apathy and sluggard indifference of our body. If we wish to acquire and utilize the power of sanctity, we must be brave in rejecting the false and temporary blandishments of the world and the flesh. Such a course of action rises above sickness and death and it takes from the body every feebleness so that in strength it can forestall the agony of death and the effects of advancing age. Our faculties are made strong even in the face of a certain decrepitude. This can be reinforced by prayer which shapes all things in love, the bracing force, and when death does arrive it is found to be the dawn of divine peace.

The recurrence of bodily pains, the frequent headaches, the soreness induced by our exertions, the constant nagging inconveniences of a broken limb — all of these need a daily, fresh intention to turn our minds and wills toward God. These are not mere reminders of our frailty, our dependence on our Creator. They are not God-given penances to help us subdue our rampant, insidious inclinations. These are the helps that our bodies need to aid us to overcome our lusts and noxious longings which keep our natural bodies from acquiring, keeping, and sustaining a healthful spirit. Pains or human sorrows are intended for our good if only we use them to increase our spiritual energies. Each can help us most beneficially to turn our minds and wills Godward.

Pains and sorrows may be the consequences of willful neglect, even serious weakness. But with patience we can cause them to serve us by increasing our strength, by making us "lean more heavily" upon our God. They can be the very means of attaining heroic strength to counteract our less than heroic response to life. We can employ pain and sorrow to our advantage.

Francis Thompson gave us encouragement in this when he wrote "To foster the energies of the body, yes, and to foster also the energies of the will that is the crying need of our uncourageous day. There is no more deadly prevalent heresy than the mechanized theory which says 'You are what you are, and you cannot be otherwise', linked with it is the false and slovenly charity which pleads 'We are all precious scoundrels in some fashion so let us love one another' — the fraternity of criminals, the brotherly love of convicts. That only can come out of a man which was in a man; but the excessive can be pruned, the latent be educed; and this is the function of the will. The will is the lynch-pin of the faculties. . . I believe that the weakest man has will enough for his appointed exigencies, if he but develop it as he would develop a feeble body. To that special end, moreover, are addressed the sacramental means of the Church. But it is also terribly true that the will, like the bodily thews, can be atrophied by indolent disuse; and at the present time numbers of men and women are suffering from just this malady, 'I cannot' waits upon 'I tried not.'"

It is for humans to make of their infirmities, even their lapses of nature, a springboard of charity — of love of self, of God, of others who suffer like afflictions. There is no waste in nature, the body adapts, can be rehabilitated, likewise the soul can be given a spiritual injection, so to speak. It will acquire a greater love and a greater response to the love that is about us like a gentle, soothing hand. Nature may abhor any infringement upon its action, any slight ascetic restraint, but even the impairments of the body serve to increase our appreciation of and need for love, for charity. Our bodies may thus be helpmates to the powers of the soul. Kahil Gibran wrote: "Your pain is the breaking of the shell that encloses your understanding" (*The Prophet*).

It is like being new-born when we seek and find our second gift of the Holy Spirit, *knowledge*. Until we seize this gift, all our steps, it seems, are like those of small toddlers, wavering, falling down, and getting up only probably to fall once more. We try again and again and take the outstretched hands of others. With strength and renewed exertion, we correct our missteps and faltering ways. The way of learning is not easy but its rewards are great. What we learn, with stumblings and aches, is greater than the experiences themselves. The beauty of the rose may be diminished by the painful prick of its thorns. But this gift of knowledge adds to our happiness by the correct management of the temporal and spiritual events of our lives, and it makes for a lighted way to mature lives, saintly lives.

One sure reward, one strength of this acquisition of the gift of knowledge, is that it is meant to aid you, lift you up, not oppress you. Yet at the same time it will give you mastery — like the increasing tension of a machine on which you strengthen your muscles. To have this gift of knowledge is to become exuberant — not in simple motion, but with focused attention to the needs and values of life.

Knowledge is the first faltering toward sanctity. It gives people a first evaluation, an inkling of their dignity and worth as individuals. It most assuredly prompts the virtue of humility. And it makes society strong by providing for the new generation the truths already harvested so that learning may advance. It is only the songbird that has the notes of joy without the struggle of learning.

Together with this lesson of humility, this gift of knowledge also has an added strength, that of love that reaches outward. Mother Therese does not have to endure all the trials of the unwanted, the dispirited, the suffering in order to help them. No, she has declared it is love, the transcendent power that recognizes the worth of those in need of another's love, and she is the conduit of the love of God made manifest in lowly actions. It is her recognition of love that enables her to serve the needy, to dispel the smoke of despair and quiet the dust that troubled feet have stirred. To allay fears and satisfy the needs of another is to show love in action; to grant peace of heart is to invigorate.

In our age of much calculating, where few people measure true value, where with abundance of pleasure there is so little joy, where there is such high fashion and such low esteem, we need to receive another gift of the Holy Spirit: this is the gift of *understanding*.

Without understanding the visible things about us remain unclear, clouded. We cannot see even our own worth, our own value. Knowledge alone cannot sustain us for no matter how vast it becomes, how high it soars, it must humbly stoop to enter the gateway of all understanding.

We seek a course that can be followed to make life easier, give solace to the soul, along the way that everyone must go. Regardless of the grasp one might have of the world's knowledge, the way is still fraught with the barbs of pain, the bloodied footsteps of sorrow. Everyone learns that the first shaft of evil when hurled has a boomerang effect, it curves back upon the hurler. The frenzy of unwise passion and indulgence, the flame of conscience squelched with each sinister cloud of folly, even the blame we would put upon another — all become as salt on wounds, gall in every draft. Each unwise, thoughtless act proves traitorous and pulls us, drugged, into the nets and chains of weaknesses that bind us helplessly to what even the physical body must cry out against in agony.

It is here, in the rescuing gift of understanding, that the mind reins to a halt and turns away from folly. The houndstooth of sin and its pain can turn into a flashing bolt of light that lets us see rightly the calamity around us and delivers us from the battering and pain our thoughtless actions have caused us.

We will discover with joy that the jagged stones of every pathway can be softened and made smooth by understanding, as we begin to see the heights from which we have fallen. Understanding lets us keep a clear course, an on-compass reading to achieve our goal. Now our very pains become the healing balm that renews our will and enables us to see the fixed star of our destination. It helps us to perceive that no one can fax himself or herself into heaven.

Why did we engage in folly? Why would we ever, even once, attempt to desecrate the truths incised into the living texture of our being? We can only wonder and try to understand the virtues, the strengths, that are really ours by using them to our advantage. We put out the specters of faults and evils that haunt us when we seek and use the gift of understanding. We rout despair and failure with the clean, clear shafts of understanding, true arrows in the quiver of our mind.

The rushing thoughts, our firm resolves, will be hurried through the turnstiles of our days and nights when we speed them with love of God and neighbor. When we use the gift of understanding to set aright our marshalled forces, our strengths in all our actions, then we can soar with wide wings of desire toward our individual fulfillment. It is then we can hurl our silence into the spheres of joyous song, rise above the mountain-tops, and make of our tears the rushing waters to turn the mill-wheels of our love for God. The glory and the light and the green ecstacy of completeness in our lives will beckon us surely to eternal fulfillment. This final gain may be seen from even the mounting pile of our human losses.

There is in every person a reaching out, an extension of the mind's tentacles, into what is not known. We all grasp for what is just beyond our thought, we probe the unknown sometimes more assiduously than we strive to unravel the known. It is our curious nature, but more, it is the inquisitiveness of the soul, insights beguile it, somehow satisfy it, and further inspire it to seek deeper into the spiritual realm which is our true home. We try to understand by enlarging the area to be understood. St. Bernard writes "Thus understanding and love, that is the knowledge of and delight in the truth, are, as it were, the two arms of the soul, with which it embraces and comprehends with all saints the length and breadth, the height and depth, that is the eternity, the love, the goodness, and the wisdom of God" (*Letters*).

St. Thomas calls the gift of understanding a "super-natural light which allows us to penetrate more deeply into those things, those shadowy recesses, where natural light and gifts fail us. It enables us to see that we may believe more firmly, love more completely, and respond more assuredly." For us it is the springboard of faith, the launching pad of all our hopes, the empyrean source of our love. This gift of the Holy Spirit is the true font of our response to God's tremendous love.

A beam of sunlight, fragments of songs, the glimpse of a smile, a hard won achievement — all of these may stand in our inner chamber of precious moments where we have our delights. To assemble these and to coalesce them all into the bright glory of our waking hours brings us *wisdom*, the gift of the all-ness of nothing and the nothingness of all.

We treasure the pleasant, happy things of living — we gather these into garlands of beauty that warm the heart and enchant the soul. These endearments serve to clear away the mists from the mirror image of ourselves. Seeing clearly, peacefully, we begin to move toward wisdom, that brings us solace, wisdom that lifts us from the wretchedness of our own mistakes.

It is in wisdom that we humans can be exultant. It lets us see the vision beyond our natural eyes. It enables us to see the splendor of reality deeper than the clouded dreams that ever flicker in the shadows of our minds. Wisdom is our true nobility, making us beloved of God, and able to extend love to Him, our neighbors, and to all others.

It is through wisdom that we comprehend the firmness and strength of our hope. Looking about us we can see clearly the uselessness of building ziggurats of folly and vanity. There are mountains of greed to be climbed, but wisdom tells us their summits are not worth our effort.

Our vanity leads us to speculate about the future. Will the righteous rise higher than we can rise, or will the wicked fall lower than we may fall? We live the present in the light of the past, and the brightness of others' lives shows the path ahead. And will our light be able to brighten the future? Who among us will build the cathedrals to stable our steeds of light, to structure those buttressed paeans of human glory, those stone hallelujahs that make hearts and minds sing? Who will write the modern psalms to resound in the tents of our minds, lift the spirits and please the ears of the saints?

What we do to assure the future in time for ourselves and our descendants can only be the result of prayer and application. Surely we know it will not be an assemblage of micro-chips extending into the beyond. Will the popular songs, the rock-and-roll orgies of synthesized noise and doggerel serve as our psalms of today to inspire those who will come after us? Surely the frightful shredding of silence will not evolve into a legacy of beauty to enrich the mind and soul — none of these will be a worthy tribute to God the Creator. Nor will any of these serve as prayer and promise given to our God, bringing exultation and consolation to the minds and hearts of the human progeny.

Only by the use of the gift of wisdom shall we rise above to overcome the confusions of the present world. By this exercise of strength, by this gift of wisdom, may we humanly aspire to our ideal of a democratic federation of governments, to a true recognition of religion that warrants a plenary constant and ordered living. It is only through wisdom that we clutch the hem of truth, clinging to the hope of higher things.

It is wisdom that broadens us and leads us to know Christ, to find all the brightness, the beauties of life, the human aspirations absorbed into the one Brightness of Being that we know as our Creator-God. We can with wisdom emerge with all the earth energies integrated into worthy life, one humankind that will assure social growth and attainment of heaven for everyone. Wisdom might be likened to a rudder that gives humanity the steady direction and the final safe harbor of glory in union with God.

Next the gift of counsel calls for a variety of exercises for it is made up of many aspects. At first glance it would seem simple, a slight addition to what has already developed within us. But counsel calls for much more, and the first of these is perseverance, application, and use. No one flexes a muscle without some effort. One does not attempt a diet without the realization that it requires personal effort — no one can diet for someone else, at least to accomplish the intent of the diet.

So while counsel seems to be other-directed, it begins with applying the exercise to oneself. St. Augustine said "What is wrong with us? What is this that you heard? The unlearned arise and take heaven by force, and here are we with all our learning, stuck fast in flesh and blood! Is there any shame in following because they have gone before us; would it not be a worse shame not to follow at once?" (*Confessions*). What the good saint meant was that everyone has an exemplar, a model, one to whom we look up and would like to follow in a good routine, one who shows the way. We cannot follow if we do not have leaders. This is even true in aerobics, a director sets the sequence of actions for others to imitate.

Of course the primary, the first person to be followed, is certainly not oneself. Most of the stumblings in life, we can all admit, take place because we fail in some way. We know what it is to "mess up," to botch what we are attempting to do. But if we observe and apply what we have learned, we can acquire skills we hardly believed we could possess.

And most assuredly the first exemplar for everyone is Christ the Lord. It is in Him that we are confirmed in the truth, made able to exercise our faith to our benefit and eternal glory. Christ said quite flatly and clearly, "Learn of Me!" It is Christ who we learn to receive and who gives the love that we each reflect. Love, if it is not warmed in the divine fires of Love Itself, must forever remain inadequate.

This is the first personal use of counsel: be wise for yourself, then you can be wise for others about you and apply the love of neighbor effectively. Then regard the saints who have preceded us. They form the phalanx of sanctity, from them we take counsel for our own great gain. It is to the extent that we see Christ in all saints that their lives become exemplars for us to follow. But we should not read or study the lives of other saints unless we are willing to read Christ's life in our own. We can see in the account of another saint only the amount of Christlike qualities that the saint made his own and therefore can reflect to others. We look to the saints and try to emulate them in the degree of the love of Christ they possessed.

We do not just recall the saints' lives as some kind of borrowed glory — memory is too shallow a grave for the saint in heaven. As for ourselves, our names may not be recorded in the pages of future books, maybe the book of time has not caught up with the list of one's worthy deeds and noble works. But all of us would like to have a saint's banner waving in memory of us in the fair fields of heaven, the pennant of glory. The aim of all sanctity is the redemption of the soul and body and thus all our efforts should be exercised to that end.

One aspect of counsel is that it becomes an effective force for us to bring others to the way of love. Each one of us can become an exemplar. For every ounce of muscle we exercise, we should expect a like amount of virtuous behavior in response. It is folly to even try to think if one is physically brainless, but we can expect results if we really apply our grace of counsel — no writer finds words of truth by merely watching the inkwell.

The popular books that document the lives of our contemporaries frequently only chronicle their weaknesses and not their virtues. Descriptions of the fool, a catalogue of follies, is the meat of today's gossip. It is the confusion and aimlessness of these lives that should frighten us all from following their aberrant ways.

Remember that we become the exemplar to our neighbor in the love we reflect. Love is the many splendored thing, the thing most find difficult to live up to every moment. It is so difficult to admit that love is as deep a mystery as pain is, as the poet wrote, "For all can feel the God that smites, but ah, how few the God that loves!" (F. Thompson, *Heaven and Hell*).

Even a saint may weep, even a saint may feel pain, and suffer the acid scar of sin. But surely the saint knows love because he has known the fire of the love of God and, like St. Francis, knows its purifying torment. When we recognize love, when we realize we are but a tear-drop in life awaiting God's sunlight to drink us unto Himself, then we can reach out in love to others.

It is for us to become a living part of the journey to God, helping, guiding, listening, pointing the way for others. We are the Ark of God's new covenant, we are His promise of fulfillment, His desire — so we must be all we can be for we are the equation of all creation made to be a saint among saints. And God entrusted us to ourselves. He put us in charge of ourselves. We are in command. Our only duty is to keep ourselves in good condition as only we can, smiling, ruby-like, full of dignity and value, strong and virtuous. Where we lead, we also go, and the road before us is clearly posted. We must be the saints God made us to be, and in love, be so for others, be their counsel.

If we wish to be strong, practice what the modern world thinks of as only weakness. If we would have a well-toned life, we must exercise our minds and wills through the gift of *piety*. The expression of love is piety. It is the moisture that makes fertile the soil of life, so that what we plant there may one day blossom. Bloom to fruit proceeds when we trust in God our Maker.

Piety is assertive. It proclaims our love. It declares that we are free to choose the highest good. It is our creed of faith, an acknowledgment of our dependence upon God, our willingness to accept the obligations of our belief.

Archbishop John Ireland said: "The timid move in crowds, the brave in single file." This is the way of piety, it affirms a position of single-mindedness and at the same time shows our adherence to what we believe in and follow as the truth. It is genuine love. With piety there is no pretense. It lays it on the line, it does not let us waver or vacillate.

In a most direct and open way, piety reflects our inward strength. It proclaims our friendship with Christ. At the same time, piety speaks of our compassion for others, our love of neighbor in our love of God. It also makes a genuine statement about our own membership in the mystical Body of Christ, and proves we are a working part. At the same time, piety bears the mark of our humility — not a cringing, scraping sort of humility, but one that squarely faces both our strengths and our weaknesses. It dissipates the illusion that we are sufficient unto ourselves for it lets us admit and recognize that we are a willing branch, taking nourishment, strength, and grace from the Vine that is Christ.

We can fly away from all the allures of evil when we firmly acknowledge that we are Christ's — God within and God without. We can each of us send the world to the threshing floors and flail away the chaff of its conceits to expose the strong fibers that feed the soul. We can in sure strength, in certain virtue, move toward the promised reward of love fulfilled. Our petty weaknesses are not armor against the onslaught of the dark — we need to follow the "Light of the world" and know that in that brightness our footsteps are secure.

We must be ourselves — we must not count the longings of others, but know that all joys are for ourselves when we use our many graces and strengths to seize heaven itself. Sometimes sin apparently smiles on us and we are beguiled into weakness, but we may still grasp the trailing strings and draw ourselves up again by penitential effort to our souls' fulfillment. Even our nights of darkness are penetrated with the fire-fly lights of God's love and we can bloom once more and bear the fruits of that love into eternity.

One thing we can be certain of amid all the doubts and allurements of this world — we are not unknown in the lovely halls of heaven. We are treasured there always like the wine is known to the decanter and its flavor speaks of the gentle wine-press that is an ancient symbol for our Savior. Even as a bird's feather in the grass is stirred by the wind and we still can see the bird's winging flight. Even as its twitter and song can be heard if we listen, so we know the love that sustains us and we thrill to future harmonies to be heard where all Love dwells.

The gold on the psalter cover will not shine more brightly to light our way to heaven, for it does not even reflect the worship and love that we give as a person of faith. For we must know as we breathe that we need to acknowledge and give homage to Him whose beckoning hand ever motions us to himself. Love reaches out to love with openness that is genuine and guileless. We can be certain that if the very air remembers our passage through it, He who made the air knows our comings and goings, and is aware of us in His atmosphere, His world.

It is an immortal hand that is laid upon our hearts, a hand that holds us through the brightness of day and the darkness of night. It is a hand of love that tethers us to the edge of heaven. Could we really think that our desire could be for less when we were molded by the saving will of God? How foolish not to strain every fiber of our hearts and minds to follow the desire that is formed within us like the instinct that guides the homing pigeon safely across the wastelands of the world.

Saintdom, rising up before the lightly guarded walls of eternity, is ours for the trying. The armor and weapons are at our disposal — we must use them all. We shake the sacramental trees, eat often of their preferred fruit; with faith in God's presence and His love, we savor often the eucharistic goodness and take in the great strength that will enable us to be a God-willed saint forever.

Everything we do energetically in the daily course of living, we can put to work for our God-willed intention. Lay the revels of our lives, with the prayers of our souls, at the feet of the redeeming Savior and not even tears will take away our joy. Accept our crosses and make redemptive strength of our weakness. Admit our needs in all humility and trust that we will be filled with the necessary graces to fulfill our God's desire for us. The frets and trials each of us must endure will be only like mist in a chilled atmosphere. And peace will be the warmth that lingers to define God's grace for us.

For many of us there will be no fame, no fortune, no laurels, but let others grieve for the unseen fame and laurels. Even the blind will see our glory and our triumph carved into eternal love fulfilled forever with our Creator in heaven. His castle, our castle; His glory, our glory; His love, our love. What we see dimly now, hidden in the darkest dark, will be seen then in fierce bright beauty, resplendent in our Creator's face.

There are things in life that we all must learn to recognize — either to avoid them or to embrace them for our own good. As an example, if we walk down a dark street at night, we may feel uneasy, we may even be filled with fear. We may be tempted to hesitate and turn back. We hear hurried footsteps behind us and we feel panic — but when we recognize the footsteps of a known friend who is approaching, calling our name, we smile, we are assured, and our fears disappear like the morning mist. It is recognition, awareness, and acceptance of the known reality that makes us strong and confident, again.

Thus the exercise of the gift of *fear of the Lord* can become the most important strength we may have for living in the security of love. In the book of Proverbs, we read an important lesson for there we are told "The fear of the Lord is the beginning of knowledge; wisdom and instruction fools despise" (Prv. 1:7). But this is not a cringing fear, a fright caused by the unknown. No, this is more reasonably named *reverence* for the Lord. It is a recognition of our own weakness and at the same time an acknowledgment of the source of our many strengths. From this reverence there flows a torrent of learning. We learn discipline, the strength of the love of God. We learn the necessary lesson of *acceptance*. We learn to accept and use the numerous goods that God showers upon us and, more importantly, the ills and pains which He permits in our lives. To became adept in this exercise of the gift of the fear of the Lord is important because it is a potent force to have on our side whether we struggle or dance through life.

In spite of grief and pain, and disappointments of the moment, there is a distant sound of promising joy as we merrily go to our eternal home. It is wise for us to learn for ourselves the lesson: be of the elect, be hopeful of the promised reward, we can be one of the eternal happy ones who possess Love in all its glory. Let the music of life be the score that our hearts play as we dance our way back to God. It was our Creator-God who struck the first melodious notes from the bell-tower of our souls and promised us contentment of mind and peace of heart in the everlasting harmonics of heaven. And for us, even the plucked strings of pain add to that special symphony of years fulfilling God's will, echoing in our soul the blessed sounds of the angel chorus. We learn that we are able to go singing to the promised beat of His loving heart. As Cardinal Newman said, "He alone is sufficient for the heart who made it" (*Miscellanies*).

It is this wonderful lesson of living that we learn from practicing the gift of fear of the Lord. In the past we said, "they charged me with the care of the vineyards: my own vineyard I have not cared for" (Sg. 1:6). And now we are able to say: "my vineyard is at my own disposal" (Sg. 8:12). It is from this strength that we gain the assurance for "the last word, when all is heard: Fear God and keep his commandments, for this is man's all; because God will bring to judgment every work, with all its hidden qualities, whether good or bad" (Eccl. 12:13).

God wrote the book — it is His book — and it tells of life and love, and both are His for He created both. We only read the words of life's salvation — our own God-given book. It is our lesson, it is our record, our biographic entity, and if we read it carefully, we too will learn of love, of truth, and having learned, we will find our way back to God, to His love, to His reward. And in the end we shall possess the wondrous book of God.

Consider God's providence, how far it ranges, from the twigs and grasses for the swallow's nest to those lesser things of gold and diamond crystal that beguile human vanity. So much we have been given, so much is ours from His bounty, the lustrous trappings of our earthly thrones to the very stones that pave the way to tombs. The lavish and the sublime are ours, but all are sands of time in the hour-glass of our lives. Those sands fall in cascades to that ocean of love which we shall possess someday.

It is great wisdom to give serious attention to the final great reward prepared for each of us. We package ourselves for heaven. We make our own label and send ourselves with love to love. At the dawn of death let us not be a rejected parcel, a misdirected bundle. One that was intended for glory, one we somehow failed to deliver but instead deflected to a final, horrible destination. We can live the life fulfilled as we were intended to live it. We go our way, or rather His way, with the prospect of heaven beckoning. There is no alternate road except one of our own making. God gives us the sign-posts and points to the destination — if we lose our way to Him, it is we who choose to turn aside.

God-our Father—
touched by
your hand
our world
is holy

7 When we have built ourselves up to sanctity, made ourselves fit for sainthood, we are still only partly
prepared to go the distance in the race of life. We must
once and for all recognize that we are dependent beings.
Some have thought that we are something like God-made
puppets, at the end of a string swinging down from heaven
— but the string does not pull us back to heaven. No, we
must climb back up that string using all of our prayerful
strength, finding the spiritual way to climb. The modern
person too often thinks that he has found the nuggets of
satisfaction in the world. The great self-delusion of our
times is in trying to hug to ourselves the pleasure and

material things we have acquired and thinking we have found the perfect means to attain our end. But this delusion of certain survival is a handful of dust if it is not refined and purified through prayer and love.

We are people of faith. As we believe in our life and death, we also believe in our resurrection, not only because Christ rose, but also because we are people of the promise of God. Therefore we act as St. Paul advises: "The fact is that whether you eat or drink — whatever you do — you should do all for the glory of God" (I Cor. 10:31). The whole created world awaits the revelation of the sons of God, and we groan and await our own resurrection (cf. Rm. 8:22ff).

Ever the most ancient and profound question is asked, why did God make us? And ever and always the answer is to know Him, to serve Him and to love Him — and it follows as the climax of the act of creation that each one of us is salvifically called to be happy with our Creator-God in heaven and for eternity. Science cannot give an answer nor assure a reward — even though we think we will be able to make our own heaven on earth. What a feeble effort, what a self-deluding golden mist, for we can only make a house of cards with no hope of permanence. Our idea is a delusion for there is only one heaven of eternal reality beckoning us, only one having the promise of being possessed forever. As St. Paul tells us: "None of us lives as his own master and none of us dies as his own master. While we live we are responsible to the Lord and when we die we die as his servants. Both in life and in death we are the Lord's" (Rm. 14:7).

It is this recognized truth that encourages us to live for

Christ and in imitation of Him. We admit our dependence upon God as our Creator. For us this is faith applied, this is hope applied, this is love applied. This is the salvific will of God fulfilled!

Because God made us, and we recognize our dependence on Him, we also recognize what wondrous things God has made for us. These things we use or abuse along our path back to him. The looms of the earth weave vernal green loveliness before our eyes and marvelous creatures live there, but too often we cast its beauty and goodness onto the dust-heaps of selfish neglect. All our senses are enchanted with the richness of creation that shines around us like the luminous glow of angel's wings.

Yet we do not appreciate all that grows in the garden of our Creator-God, and we even sow the weeds of our own destruction among the blossoms of His generous glory. We weave ungratefulness into the tattered, harsh cloth of our lives. We have so many God-given materials and benefits to work with — why do we so often produce only our own selfish ugliness? Why do we not return love to Love and to Bounty be bountiful? The raiment of our life should be a fair and fitting garment to clothe us as we stand in sainthood before our Creator-King. We are the most blessed of all living creatures, and so we should array ourselves in our most glorious fashion — we alone can share in His glory by returning His love.

Even the most wretched of us must sometimes stand in awe before the wonders of God's creation, its beauty, its orderliness. There are no words to express the wonders that we behold. We can only murmur, "Oh, my Lord, how wonderful is all of this!" In the greenery of the forest which houses the song of birds, even the silence is a thunderous shout of God's glory. There is the thrill of scent from garden blossoms, and we see the flush of heaven's palette in the trees of autumn, the sunset's splash on the waters of a quiet lake. While we move amid such glory, how can we still ignore the spiritual glories and helps that we receive along the way? Even in the murky darkness of ignorance, in the ordinary everyday nowness of living, God's joy is not denied us if only we turn to His love for loveliness. Sometimes we go our way unthinking amid the beauties that satisfy our senses in temporary surfeit. But it is a patient Creator who awaits our coming to Him. He looks for us at the gates of happiness in His wondrous halls of eternal beauty.

Simplicity of life is possible when we recognize our dependence upon the bountiful handouts of a most generous God. And how do we acknowledge this bounty, these gifts? It is by what we do with these gifts to fulfill the will of God for us. Everything created is made for the glory of God. Now we know that God has "all glory." He needs nothing further to be given to Him. But in creating all things and beings, God intends all for glory, that is, to be included or embraced within that glory which is God, Himself.

We can best be aware of our obligation to our Creator by (1) prayer; (2) being like Christ in all things; (3) gratitude that is best shown by worship of God; and (4) our acceptance of life's sufferings and pain for the love of God. These often appear to be quite foreign to modern men and women, and they are always repugnant to the selfish and lazy. Lessons about virtues seldom touch today's sybarites who have draped themselves with the veils of every sensual indulgence. The obligation we owe to a most benevolent God is a very opaque idea for some modern people. But they do know, sometimes from hard-won experience that one cannot grow lovely vegetables and beautiful flowers from a compost of flesh and fat and golden baubles. Education, the refinement of culture and moral values alone will assure the cultivation of nobility in us. With maturity education is seen to be the bearer of beauty, solace, and order to our nature, and our world. Today has its mad combination of fantasies that portray this life as best realized by the petty, clay-bound, unworthy rewards of society.

Prayer, then, is the first response of a dependent, loving, and grateful creature to his Maker. It is the pre-eminent effective means of sanctification, an open door to sainthood. St. Paul tells us "Never cease praying, render constant thanks, such is God's will for you in Christ Jesus" (I Thes. 5:7). This response arises naturally from your faith, to ignore it is to weaken and fall by the wayside.

We can easily comprehend that all creatures must and do give glory to God. The psalmist proclaims "The heavens declare the glory of God, and the firmament proclaims his handiwork" (Ps. 19:2). And St. Paul confirms our knowledge and duty: "For from him and through him all things are. To him be glory forever. Amen" (Rm. 11:36). And Paul notes our dependence: "While we live we are responsible to the Lord, and when we die we die as his servants" (Rm. 14:8). Further, we must do the things of ourselves to be like Christ and glorify God in our bodies (cf. I Cor. 6:20).

Most notable of our responses to a generous God is the love that we show by trying to keep ourselves worthy of accepting His love poured out to us. St. Francis de Sales said "The love of men toward God takes its being, progress, and perfection from the eternal love of God toward men" (*Treatise on the Love of God*). It is an obligation which is ours when we are created, and one to which we respond with reverence. And if we exercise the gift of piety from the Holy Spirit, then we will train ourselves "for a life of piety" (I Tm. 4:7). This requires a daily commitment, first, to begin and end each day by placing ourselves in close relationship to God and, second, to spend at least a short period of every day addressing God in prayer.

There is a final grace note to our prayer of gratitude. That is, that we express our thanks even when we ask for something more. Our prayers of petition show that we recognize God as Source of our goodness and are confident that if we need more to encourage us, we simply ask and it will be given to us. St. John reminds us: "We have this confidence in God that he hears us whenever we ask anything according to his will. And since we know that he hears us whenever we ask, we know that what we have asked him for is ours" (I Jn. 5:14). This again points to our trusting dependence on God, the fountain of all blessings.

Most worthy of all our actions as Christians is the worship of God alone, God before us, God in us, and with us in all of our living. Pope Pius XI wrote "Human society as such is bound to offer to God public and social worship. It is bound to acknowledge in Him its supreme Lord and first beginning, and to strive toward Him as to its last end, to give Him thanks and offer Him propitiation." And the author Gerald Vann puts it bluntly, "Worship, then, is not a part of the Christian life; it is the Christian life" (*The Divine Pity*).

Some would say that imitation is the greatest flattery, but we in imitating Christ fulfill the highest duty of religion, the worship of God. We make humble obeisance as a creature before our Creator, and show our love for Him.

One of the most difficult lessons we all must learn, perhaps by the concerted effort of our bodies, our minds and our wills, is that there is a time inevitably when we suffer pain or loss. This is not just a lesson for our good, it is the distinct manifestation of God's special love. If we cannot or will not use the disciplines, the treadmills of pain, of sinlessness, of arduous virtues, then we may still go to the God of tenderness and love, to Him who alone will accept our offerings of inadequacy. But if we are resolved to climb the mountain of holiness to be forever with Love, then know that we must endure the cresting pains that guard the gates of the heavenly summit. Once we have faced with fortitude of mind and heart the bleak realities of life, we gather confidence to complete the struggle, the exercise of life, for "this means that you are strangers and aliens no longer. No, you are fellow citizens of the saints and members of the household of God" (Eph. 2:19). For we learn from life that one who suffers also conquers and that a world we would have free of sorrow would also be more frightfully, a world without joy.

What brings man closer to man, to the real neighborliness, that we call love? It is often a sadness arising out of some calamity, some tragedy that is visited upon someone causing pain and earning our response of sorrow. Without this response, there would be no brotherliness, no companionship in suffering, no compassion. Sadness is like a condiment, the herbal fragrance that gives savor to our expressions of love. We are all hungry for the sustaining food of compassion. Grief is often a bond that binds us in love, even as our Redeemer was sorrowful unto death — the death that was radical proof of love eternal.

Sometimes we are like Solomon who, the more he learned, the more sorrowful he became. In our mourning we learn greater wisdom, we can overcome the ignorance of weakness and by experience know love more fully. We reap the rewards of sadness only when we can weep out of love. Being brave in the face of afflictions is foolish only when we fail to make them salutary.

It is our way of going in love to Love — our souls are ever hungry for the sweet meats of living, though these have a price. We can blame the time in which we live where there is so much pleasure with so little joy, so much learning and science with a paucity of wisdom. It is certainly futile to shake the tree strenuously and then neglect to reap the fruits. So many profess to scholarly pursuits and yet we produce no philosophers, no men and women of vision, no shapers of the arts and literature. Our practical foresight and human ability are too often productive of wretched despair. So much beauty is wasted upon the barren, shifting sands of empty desires.

But it is through pain and suffering that we learn to plough the fields of our true desires, to harvest future happiness. It is thus that the favored one, St. Francis of Assisi, suffering the holy agony of the stigmata, could speak his words of praise for his Savior:

You are Love,
You are wisdom,
You are humility,
You are endurance,
You are rest,
You are peace,
You are joy and gladness,
You are justice and moderation,
You are all our riches,
And you suffice for us.
                              —The Praises of God

In today's world there is a strange dichotomy. On the one hand, we have widespread killing of the unborn and on the other, a fierce seeking after longevity of life. The unborn cast shadows on the flowers of pleasure, and the aged face a wall of fears of the unknown. Perhaps this arises from a great reverse confusion between the idea of life as a purposeful seeking for the perfection of all humans, and the destroying of any hope of such perfection. There is a selfish use of what many believe is their only resource: time. They believe it is theirs alone to use, control, to waste or save. To stretch out this valuable time, people try new cults, a mysticism of health and bodily well-being, a temporizing relief in soul-deadening drugs. There is a desperate ignorance that tries to console itself with delusions of reincarnation or the mind-maddening search among the occult. Who can measure the depth of a dried-up river or pick out shadows from the mind's darkness?

There is in these pursuits, a rejection of the true purpose of life which has only one ultimate desire, to satisfy the human soul. This is the deep truth of all living, the seeking of salvation, of eternal happiness. The Christian belief, the revealed assurance of Christ, of God himself, often eludes many because they refuse to admit or accept the blessed helps that have been offered. To them faith is folly, and restraint or self-denial is madness. They even refuse to acknowledge the demonstrated reality of a commerce between body and spirit, mind and soul, the true psychology of living.

There have been recent demonstrations to prove that the forces of the soul do have a sovereign rule over the body, that the spirit enforces the flesh, that the mind can overcome bodily weaknesses. It has even been acknowledged that sanctity is medicinal, that virtue exercised increases virtue's strength. It is like a beneficial steroid that makes stronger not larger, the muscles of the body and soul. Some say it is simply mind over matter, but before that can be an effective course to follow, there must be prayer over malice and weakness — prayer that is the dawning of interior peace. It is even found that the love of God, and the attendant necessary love of neighbor, is the pre-eminent ethical sanity that makes life peaceful and joyful. Virtue practiced lifts its own weight and unburdens even the reluctant body. Weakness of the body, lapses of the will or mind, have often been found to take strength from the energizing force of holiness. This recognition of the bonding power of soul and body takes away the paralysing feebleness that prevents us from seeking our true sanctity in Love through love.

All these lessons are evident in the experiences of the divorced, the dope-befuddled, the sexually weary, and the ravaged self-indulgent. We can all learn the lessons and profit from the sad examples. Some lessons are sorely learned, gained with much more pain than the denial of our petty wants and whims would ever cause.

Those who place their mortal weakness, their sagging wills, on some road of ascetical recovery find a new purpose, a new light. At the first clap of the bell of awakening, a new peace of mind and heart will spring up with renewed vitality. When we learn that even the smallest step in an effort to be holy energizes and restores vigor, we will find the energy to overcome "brother donkey" and even ride our fragile mounts to a more rewarding life.

Renewed youth and strength are the surprising fruits of self-denial, prayer, and the full use of the grace of God to seek perfection, to be saints. It is thus that all humans can fulfill the salvific will of God who wishes their attainment of eternal glory.

The creative hand of God, as pictured in Michelangelo's painting in the Sistine Chapel, is ever reaching out to touch our outstretched hands. He is always beckoning, always waiting, always smiling His eternal welcome, and always saying to us: "Clasp my hand and come into the glory that I have prepared for you from the very beginning!"

We are all, each one of us, led by love. We belong to Love. Our bodies may deteriorate because of the burdens we have borne, because of our failures and our impaired constitution and will, but always one strength of love remains — we can still weakly reach out and pull down the neck of our Creator and embrace forever the glory that is eternally His. "Peace be with you!" we hear, and accept the soothing sound through love fulfilled.

We will each walk the pathways of nature, climb the

mortal stairways to the highest meadows of lovely blossoms, sound the depths and heights where all beauties and songs blend into the eternal vision where even death forgets to die. There we will shout our joy from the peaks of space and sound the tranquil harmony on the winds of our contentment.

When we meet at last the Eternal Fair, we will be swallowed up in the embrace of Love where all of our nature can revel without restraint. This is for us all the eternal terminus, the depot of delight where we are melded into the communion of saints. We will see our mother, Queen of Heaven, in the crystal clarity of her beauty, hear the angelic cloud of song, receive the hand of God who lovingly encircles us in eternal glory.

It is sanctity at last for each of us, the crown for all efforts. It is sanctity; we attain our wish for ourselves and the others we have encountered along the way. It is our everlasting song of alleluia! In the presence of this glorious galaxy, we may feel powerless, yet, in our human frailty there is a dignity which is not of ourselves but of God. It is His immanence, His presence that overwhelms us. It is not a built-in strength, rather it is like the ambiance of song, of truth, that one lives in even after the song is stilled, and when we face the truth starkly before us. The after-echo, the remembered harmonious sound forms an aureole about us. It is our own reflection of the glory of God. It is a torrent of beauty that inundates us completely.

Our response to God today is in recognition that love generates duty and a willingness to serve. It is at times the hard-to-bear pain of life that brings into focus the sweet presence of God in the world about us. Sorrow sometimes blends into sorrow and our very flesh cries out — old pain seems to incarnate new pain. It almost seems we must learn a lesson of hell before the unfolded blossom of life makes credible the promise God gave us from the beginning. We distil a river of tears that loses itself in the flood of love that gushes from the heart of God.

In the press of living we are, when we pause to think, the rich wine that comes from the joy of every day that love endures. Our ability to love is intensified by the repetition of that love as we wax stronger in experiencing God's love omni-present. Keeping always before us the beauty and splendor of our God, we will return, like a reflection in a mirror, to proclaim that Divine presence.

We are planted as a little root in the mystery soil of God and we await His harvest, His will, where divine all-Being is the focus-point of His glory and ours.

It is there, where the angel hosts keep their eager vigil of welcome, that we shall know the unknowable, and claim our promised reward. *Deus vult* - -God wills it.

Praise and Glory to God

Come, let us sing joyfully to the Lord; let us acclaim the Rock of our salvation.
Let us greet him with thanksgiving; let us joyfully sing psalms to him.
For the Lord is a great God, and a great king above all gods;
In his hands are the depths of the earth, and the tops of the mountains are his.
His is the sea, for he has made it, and the dry land, which his hands have formed.
Come, let us bow down in worship; let us kneel before the Lord who made us.
For he is our God,
and we are the people he shepherds, the flock he guides.

—Psalm 95:1-7